Lean Startup Marketing

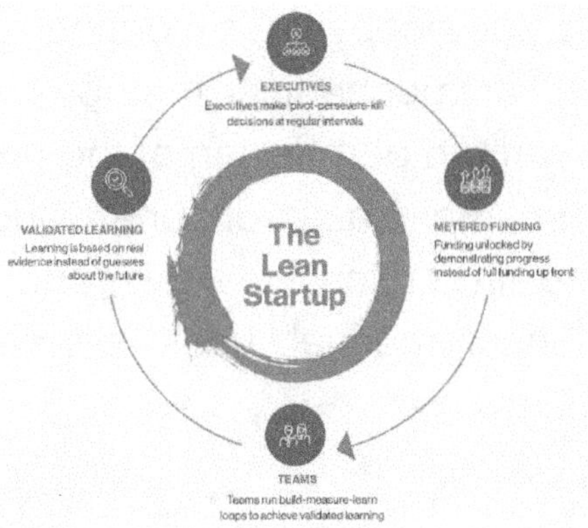

Self Proven Strategies for Agile Business Growth

LEWIS MADISON

Table of Contents

Introduction

Welcome to a transformative exploration of entrepreneurial ingenuity and strategic marketing prowess. In the dynamic realm of business, adaptability and innovation are the cornerstones of success. This introduction invites you into the world of Lean Startup Marketing, where proven strategies serve as a compass for agile business growth.

Setting the Stage for Transformation: As markets evolve and consumer behaviors shift, traditional approaches to marketing often fall short. This section illuminates the need for a paradigm shift in business strategies. Entrepreneurs and business leaders are encouraged to embrace a mindset of constant evolution and nimbleness, recognizing that the ability to pivot swiftly is a competitive advantage in the modern business landscape.

Strategies for Agile Business Growth: Beyond the confines of conventional marketing, Lean Startup Marketing introduces a set of self-proven strategies designed to catalyze growth. From innovative customer acquisition methods to the art of crafting a Minimum Viable Product (MVP), this journey unfolds as a guide to navigating the challenges of business while fostering sustainable growth.

The Intricacies of Marketing Prowess: This introduction tantalizingly hints at the wealth of knowledge to be uncovered in subsequent chapters. Readers will delve into the nuances of metrics that truly matter, scalable approaches to business expansion, and the art of building resilience in the face of uncertainties. This journey is not merely a guide; it's an invitation to master the art of marketing agility and propel your business into new dimensions of success.

Embark on a voyage where strategic innovation meets calculated risk-taking, where the rules are rewritten, and where the pulse of the market is not just observed but actively shaped. Lean Startup Marketing beckons those ready to challenge the status quo and embrace a future where sustainable business growth is not just a goal but a tangible outcome.

Understanding the Lean Startup Framework

In the ever-evolving landscape of entrepreneurship, the Lean Startup framework stands as a guiding beacon, offering a structured approach to innovation and growth. Rooted in the philosophy of continuous improvement and validated learning, this framework provides entrepreneurs and business leaders with a powerful set of tools to navigate the uncertainties inherent in the early stages of a venture.

Principles of Lean Startup: At its core, the Lean Startup framework is built upon a foundation of fundamental principles. This section meticulously dissects these principles, emphasizing the importance of rapid iteration, a customer-centric approach, and the relentless pursuit of validated learning. Entrepreneurs are encouraged to embrace a mindset that views each iteration not as a potential failure but as a valuable learning opportunity.

Build-Measure-Learn Loop: At the heart of the Lean Startup methodology is the Build-Measure-Learn loop, a dynamic cycle that propels innovation. This section provides a deep dive into each phase, elucidating how entrepreneurs can efficiently build a Minimum Viable Product (MVP), measure its impact through key metrics, and, most crucially, learn from customer feedback to iterate and improve.

Continuous Innovation: The Lean Startup framework champions the concept of continuous innovation as a means to stay ahead in a competitive landscape. This section explores the strategies that enable businesses to stay nimble, pivot when necessary, and foster a culture where adaptability is not just a choice but a necessity.

Risk Mitigation through Validation: A hallmark of the Lean Startup approach is its emphasis on risk mitigation through validated learning. Entrepreneurs are guided through the process of validating assumptions, ensuring that decisions are grounded in real-world feedback rather than speculative conjecture. This section equips readers with the tools to identify and test key hypotheses effectively.

Application Across Industries: While the Lean Startup framework originated in the tech startup sphere, its applicability has transcended industry boundaries. This section showcases real-world examples of how diverse businesses, from tech startups to established enterprises, have successfully implemented Lean principles to drive innovation, mitigate risks, and achieve sustainable growth.

As we delve into the intricacies of the Lean Startup framework, readers will not only gain a profound understanding of its principles but also acquire actionable insights to apply these principles in their own entrepreneurial endeavors. This journey is not merely a theoretical exploration; it is a roadmap for those seeking to revolutionize their approach to business, fostering a culture of innovation and resilience in the face of uncertainty.

The Crucial Significance of Lean Marketing in Business Growth

In the dynamic and competitive landscape of contemporary business, the importance of Lean Marketing cannot be overstated. As a strategic approach rooted in efficiency, adaptability, and customer-centricity, Lean Marketing emerges as a catalyst for sustained business growth, providing a roadmap for entrepreneurs to navigate the complexities of the modern marketplace.

Agility in Action: One of the key pillars of Lean Marketing lies in its emphasis on agility. Traditional marketing strategies often unfold over extended periods, rendering businesses slow to adapt to changing market dynamics. Lean Marketing, however, champions a nimble approach, enabling businesses to pivot swiftly based on real-time feedback and market insights. This agility is not merely a response to change but a proactive stance that positions businesses ahead of the curve.

Resource Optimization: Lean Marketing advocates for the efficient allocation of resources, ensuring that every marketing effort contributes directly to business objectives. This section delves into the principles of resource optimization, highlighting how Lean Marketing allows businesses to maximize the impact of their campaigns while minimizing unnecessary expenditures. From lean budgeting to prioritized efforts, this strategic allocation fosters a culture of efficiency.

Customer-Centricity at the Core: At the heart of Lean Marketing is an unwavering focus on the customer. By prioritizing customer needs and preferences, businesses can tailor their marketing strategies to resonate more effectively. This customer-centric approach is not confined to initial product development but extends throughout the marketing lifecycle, creating a feedback loop that continually refines strategies based on real-world interactions.

Rapid Iteration and Continuous Improvement: Lean Marketing borrows a page from the Lean Startup methodology, advocating for a mindset of continuous improvement through rapid iteration. This section explores how businesses can apply this iterative approach to marketing campaigns, allowing for quick adjustments based on performance metrics and customer feedback. The result is not just a one-time marketing effort but an evolving, refined strategy that aligns seamlessly with the evolving market landscape.

Data-Driven Decision Making: In an era where data reigns supreme, Lean Marketing places a premium on data-driven decision making. By leveraging key performance indicators (KPIs) and analytics, businesses can gain valuable insights into the effectiveness of their marketing efforts. This section outlines how the strategic use of data empowers businesses to make informed decisions, refine their targeting, and optimize their overall marketing strategy for maximum impact.

Building Resilience in Turbulent Times: As markets face uncertainties and disruptions, the resilience embedded in Lean Marketing becomes a strategic advantage. This section explores how businesses can build resilience by maintaining flexibility, adapting swiftly to changing circumstances, and utilizing customer feedback as a compass to navigate turbulent waters.

In essence, the importance of Lean Marketing in business growth lies not only in its theoretical principles but in its practical application as a transformative force. This strategic approach not only guides businesses through the intricacies of marketing but cultivates a mindset that positions them as dynamic, customer-focused entities ready to thrive in an ever-evolving business landscape.

Lean
Startup

Chapter 1: Foundations of Lean Startup Marketing

In the dynamic terrain of business, the foundations of Lean Startup Marketing serve as the compass that guides entrepreneurs through the complexities of modern markets. This exploration delves into the fundamental pillars that underpin agile growth and sustainable business development, shedding light on the essential elements that set the stage for marketing success.

Customer-Centric Approach: At the heart of Lean Startup Marketing lies a steadfast commitment to understanding and addressing customer needs. This section explores the intricacies of adopting a customer-centric approach, emphasizing the importance of aligning marketing strategies with the desires and pain points of the target audience. By placing the customer experience at the forefront, businesses create a solid foundation for building relationships and fostering brand loyalty.

Customer Discovery: Identifying Target Audiences: The journey begins with a deep dive into the process of customer discovery. Entrepreneurs are guided through effective methods for identifying and understanding their core customer base. This foundational step ensures that marketing efforts are not only directed towards the right audience but also resonate with the unique characteristics of that audience, setting the groundwork for impactful campaigns.

Validating Market Demand for Your Product/Service: Lean Startup Marketing thrives on the principle of mitigating risks through early validation. This section explores strategies for validating market demand, ensuring that the products or services being offered align with genuine market needs. By avoiding assumptions and leveraging feedback loops, businesses refine their offerings to meet real-world demands, fostering a strategic advantage in a landscape driven by ever-shifting consumer preferences.

Minimum Viable Product (MVP) Development:
The concept of the Minimum Viable Product (MVP)
is a cornerstone of Lean Startup Marketing. This
section delves into the art of crafting a focused and
streamlined MVP, allowing businesses to test their
hypotheses and gather valuable feedback from
early adopters. The iterative nature of MVP
development sets the stage for continuous
improvement and innovation.

As we explore these foundational elements, it
becomes evident that Lean Startup Marketing is not
just a theoretical framework but a practical guide to
navigating the intricacies of modern marketing. By
embracing a customer-centric approach, honing in
on target audiences, validating market demand,
and strategically developing MVPs, businesses
establish a robust foundation for marketing
success. These pillars serve as the building blocks
of a marketing strategy that is not only adaptable to
change but actively shapes the trajectory of
business growth in a competitive and dynamic
landscape.

Defining Lean Principles in Marketing: Crafting a Strategic Foundation

In the dynamic landscape of marketing, the adoption of Lean principles stands as a transformative force, reshaping the way businesses approach strategy, innovation, and customer engagement. This exploration delves into the core tenets that define Lean principles in marketing, offering insights into how this strategic framework becomes a compass for agile and efficient business growth.

Efficiency Through Elimination of Waste: At the forefront of Lean principles lies a commitment to efficiency achieved through the elimination of waste. This section elucidates how marketers can scrutinize their processes to identify and eradicate inefficiencies, ensuring that every effort, resource, and campaign contributes directly to business objectives. By streamlining operations, businesses not only conserve resources but create a lean, responsive marketing machine.

Continuous Improvement and Iteration: Central to Lean principles is the concept of continuous improvement. This section explores how marketers can embrace a mindset of perpetual enhancement, iterating on strategies based on real-time data and market feedback. Through this iterative approach, marketing campaigns evolve dynamically, adapting to changing market conditions and optimizing for maximum impact.

Customer-Centricity as a Guiding Principle: Lean marketing places paramount importance on understanding and fulfilling customer needs. This section delves into how businesses can adopt a customer-centric approach, ensuring that marketing strategies resonate authentically with the target audience. By empathizing with customer pain points and aspirations, businesses not only enhance brand loyalty but also position themselves as responsive entities in the eyes of the consumer.

Validation of Assumptions through Data: Lean principles emphasize the validation of assumptions through data-driven decision-making. This section explores how marketers can leverage key performance indicators (KPIs) and analytics to gain meaningful insights. By grounding decisions in empirical evidence, businesses move away from speculative strategies, reducing the risks associated with untested assumptions and ensuring a more informed and strategic marketing approach.

Cross-Functional Collaboration for Holistic Impact: Lean principles transcend siloed approaches, encouraging cross-functional collaboration for holistic impact. This section elucidates how breaking down departmental barriers fosters a collaborative environment where insights and expertise converge. The result is a marketing strategy that integrates perspectives from various disciplines, promoting innovation and adaptability.

As we define Lean principles in marketing, it becomes evident that this framework is not merely a set of theoretical concepts but a strategic guide that transforms the marketing landscape. Efficiency, continuous improvement, customer-centricity, data-driven decisions, and cross-functional collaboration collectively form the bedrock upon which businesses can build resilient, adaptive, and impactful marketing strategies. Embracing Lean principles becomes more than a choice; it is a commitment to a dynamic, responsive, and customer-focused approach that propels businesses toward sustained growth and success.

Applying Agile Methodology to Business Strategy: A Blueprint for Adaptive Excellence

In the fast-paced arena of modern business, the application of Agile methodology to business strategy emerges as a dynamic and transformative force. This exploration delves into the intricacies of how businesses can adopt Agile principles to cultivate a strategic environment that thrives on adaptability, collaboration, and iterative excellence.

Foundations of Agile Methodology: At the core of Agile methodology lies a set of principles that originated in software development but have proven universally applicable. This section meticulously dissects these principles, emphasizing the iterative development cycle, flexibility to change, and the power of collaborative, cross-functional teams. The foundations of Agile serve as the framework upon which businesses can build an adaptive, resilient strategy.

Sprint-Based Iteration: One of the hallmarks of Agile is its embrace of sprint-based iteration. This section explores how businesses can break down their strategic goals into manageable sprints, allowing for focused development and rapid adaptation. By regularly reassessing priorities and adjusting strategies based on real-time feedback, businesses foster a culture of continuous improvement, ensuring their strategies remain aligned with evolving market dynamics.

Cross-Functional Collaboration: Agile methodology champions cross-functional collaboration as a catalyst for innovation. This section delves into how breaking down traditional departmental silos fosters a collaborative environment where diverse perspectives converge. The synergy of talents from various disciplines not only accelerates decision-making but also infuses strategic planning with a richness that arises from a diversity of insights.

Embracing Change as a Constant: Agile methodology's resilience lies in its acknowledgment of change as a constant. This section explores how businesses can shift their mindset to view change not as a disruption but as an opportunity for growth. By adapting swiftly to market shifts, embracing unforeseen opportunities, and learning from setbacks, businesses position themselves as dynamic entities capable of thriving in an ever-changing landscape.

Feedback Loops for Informed Decision-Making: Agile methodology places a premium on data-driven decision-making through continuous feedback loops. This section elucidates how businesses can leverage key performance indicators (KPIs) and customer feedback to inform their strategic decisions. The iterative nature of these feedback loops ensures that strategies remain finely tuned and aligned with the evolving needs of the market and the customer.

Scaling Agile Practices: As businesses grow, the challenge lies in scaling Agile practices effectively. This section explores strategies for scaling Agile beyond individual teams, ensuring that the principles of adaptability and collaboration permeate the entire organization. By maintaining the core tenets of Agile, even in large-scale operations, businesses can sustain their agility and responsiveness.

As we navigate the realm of applying Agile methodology to business strategy, it becomes clear that this approach is not just a set of practices but a transformative philosophy. By embracing iterative development, fostering cross-functional collaboration, adapting to change, leveraging feedback loops, and scaling Agile practices, businesses forge a strategic path that is not only dynamic but resilient in the face of uncertainties. The application of Agile methodology becomes a blueprint for adaptive excellence, propelling businesses toward sustained innovation and success.

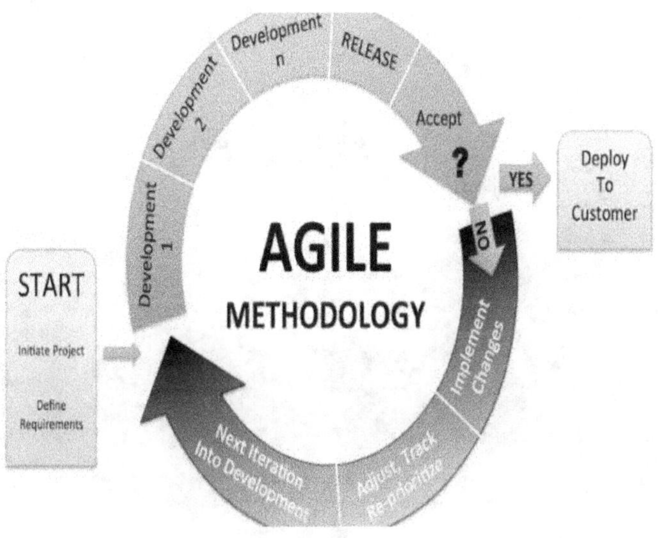

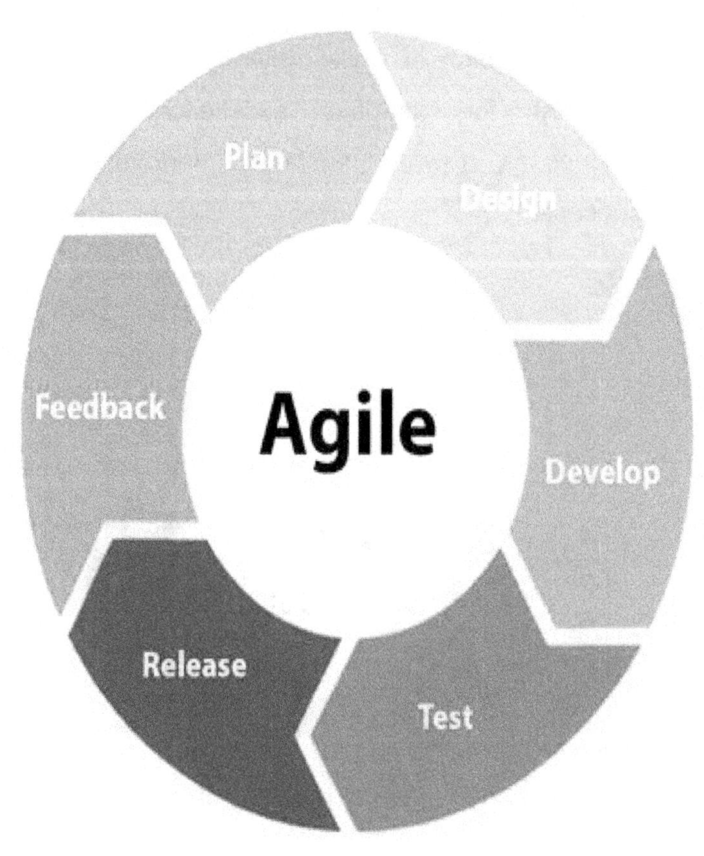

Plan
Design
Feedback
Agile
Develop
Release
Test

Chapter 2: Market Research and Validation

In the intricate dance of business, market research and validation emerge as twin pillars upon which successful strategies are built. This exploration navigates the nuanced landscape of understanding the market and ensuring the viability of offerings, shedding light on the strategic depth required for businesses to thrive in an ever-evolving environment.

Holistic Market Understanding: Market research goes beyond mere data collection; it is a holistic endeavor to comprehend the intricacies of the market landscape. This section delves into how businesses can conduct in-depth analyses, examining industry trends, competitive landscapes, and consumer behaviors. By synthesizing qualitative and quantitative data, companies gain a panoramic view that informs strategic decisions and shapes marketing initiatives.

Consumer Psychographics and Behaviors: Understanding the psyche and behaviors of consumers is at the heart of effective market research. This section explores the art of delving into consumer psychographics, unraveling not just what consumers buy but why they buy it. By deciphering the motivations, preferences, and pain points of the target audience, businesses gain a profound understanding that transcends surface-level insights, laying the groundwork for resonant marketing strategies.

Competitor Intelligence and Benchmarking: Market validation involves a strategic assessment of the competitive landscape. This section explores how businesses can conduct comprehensive competitor intelligence and benchmarking, identifying strengths, weaknesses, and unique selling propositions. By situating themselves within the market context, businesses can refine their value propositions and differentiate themselves effectively.

Emerging Trends and Future Projections: Market dynamics are ever-changing, influenced by technological advancements, societal shifts, and global events. This section navigates the process of anticipating emerging trends and projecting the future trajectory of the market. By staying ahead of the curve, businesses position themselves as proactive entities capable of adapting to evolving consumer demands and preferences.

Strategic Positioning and Brand Perception: Market research extends to the realm of strategic positioning and brand perception. This section explores how businesses can craft their brand image to align with consumer expectations and values. By fostering positive brand perceptions, companies not only attract their target audience but also establish a foundation for long-term customer loyalty.

Iterative Validation through Pilot Programs:
Validation is an ongoing process, and this section
introduces the concept of iterative validation
through pilot programs. Businesses can
strategically launch smaller-scale initiatives to test
new products, features, or marketing strategies. By
analyzing the outcomes and gathering feedback,
companies can refine their approach before a
full-scale rollout, minimizing risks and maximizing
the impact of their initiatives.

As we navigate the multifaceted realms of market
research and validation, it becomes evident that
this strategic duo is more than a checklist; it's an
ongoing dialogue with the market. By deeply
understanding the market landscape, deciphering
consumer behaviors, strategically assessing
competitors, anticipating future trends, and
iteratively validating initiatives, businesses craft a
foundation that is not only informed but resilient in
the face of market dynamics. This strategic depth
becomes the compass that guides businesses
toward sustained growth and relevance.

Customer Discovery: The Art and Science of Identifying Target Audiences

In the intricate tapestry of business success, customer discovery takes center stage as a pivotal process, providing the compass for identifying and understanding target audiences. This exploration delves into the nuanced art and science of customer discovery, unveiling the strategic depth required to connect with the right audience in an ever-evolving marketplace.

Defining Customer Discovery: Customer discovery transcends traditional market research; it is an immersive journey that seeks to understand the aspirations, pain points, and preferences of potential customers. This section unfolds the layers of customer discovery, emphasizing its role as the initial step in building meaningful connections with target audiences.

Empathy at the Core: At the heart of customer discovery lies empathy—a deep understanding of the customer's world. This section explores how businesses can cultivate empathy by stepping into the shoes of their target audience. By discerning the challenges, desires, and motivations of customers, businesses elevate their ability to resonate authentically and craft solutions that genuinely address their needs.

Persona Development: An integral component of customer discovery is the creation of customer personas. This section delves into the meticulous process of persona development, crafting detailed profiles that encapsulate the characteristics of the target audience. By personifying their ideal customers, businesses not only humanize their audience but also gain clarity on how to tailor marketing messages effectively.

Active Engagement and Dialogue: Customer discovery is not a passive exercise; it involves active engagement and dialogue. This section explores how businesses can initiate conversations with potential customers, seeking not only to gather information but also to build relationships. By fostering a two-way dialogue, companies gain insights that transcend data points, capturing the nuances of customer perspectives.

Market Segmentation for Precision: To identify target audiences effectively, businesses must embrace market segmentation. This section navigates the strategic process of dividing the broader market into distinct segments based on shared characteristics. By honing in on specific segments, businesses can tailor their offerings and messaging with precision, resonating more profoundly with the intended audience.

Feedback as a Catalyst for Innovation: Customer discovery is a continual feedback loop that catalyzes innovation. This section explores how businesses can leverage feedback from potential customers to refine their products, services, or marketing strategies. By treating feedback as a valuable resource, companies position themselves to iterate and evolve in alignment with the ever-changing needs of their audience.

Data-Driven Decision Making: Customer discovery relies on data-driven decision-making. This section elucidates how businesses can collect and analyze relevant data to inform their customer discovery efforts. By embracing metrics and analytics, companies gain a comprehensive understanding of customer behaviors, enabling them to make strategic decisions grounded in empirical evidence.

As we traverse the landscape of customer discovery, it becomes evident that this process is not merely about collecting information—it's about building relationships and understanding the human side of business. By cultivating empathy, developing detailed personas, engaging in active dialogue, embracing market segmentation, leveraging feedback, and making data-driven decisions, businesses unveil a strategic approach that transcends traditional marketing. Customer discovery becomes a dynamic journey that not only identifies target audiences but also establishes the foundation for meaningful and lasting connections with customers in a world where personalization and authenticity reign supreme.

Market Demand Validation: Navigating the Crucible of Business Assurance

In the ever-shifting landscape of commerce, the process of validating market demand for a product or service emerges as a critical crucible—one that tests the viability and potential success of an offering. This exploration delves into the intricacies of market demand validation, unveiling the strategic depth required to ensure that a product or service aligns seamlessly with the dynamic needs and desires of the market.

Understanding the Essence of Market Demand: Market demand is more than a numerical figure; it encapsulates the very essence of customer interest and acceptance. This section delves into the multifaceted nature of market demand, emphasizing the importance of going beyond quantitative metrics to discern the qualitative aspects that define genuine interest and demand.

Pilot Programs as Proving Grounds: Validation begins with strategic initiatives such as pilot programs. This section explores how businesses can strategically launch smaller-scale versions of their products or services to test the waters. By analyzing the outcomes and gathering feedback in a controlled environment, companies gain valuable insights that inform further development and refinement before a full-scale launch.

Customer Feedback as a North Star: The heartbeat of market demand validation lies in customer feedback. This section elucidates how businesses can create mechanisms for actively seeking and analyzing customer input. By treating feedback as a guiding light, companies navigate the intricate nuances of customer preferences, allowing them to tailor their offerings with precision.

Iterative Adaptation and Improvement: The process of market demand validation is inherently iterative. This section explores how businesses can adapt and improve their offerings based on the insights garnered from initial launches. By embracing a mindset of continuous improvement, companies position themselves to respond dynamically to evolving market dynamics, ensuring their products or services stay relevant.

Strategic Pricing Experiments: Pricing plays a pivotal role in market demand validation. This section navigates the strategic terrain of pricing experiments, exploring how businesses can test different pricing models to gauge customer responsiveness. By aligning pricing structures with perceived value, companies gain a deeper understanding of how the market values their offerings.

Competitor Analysis for Benchmarking: A robust validation strategy involves analyzing the competitive landscape. This section explores how businesses can conduct thorough competitor analysis, benchmarking their offerings against similar products or services in the market. By understanding where they stand in relation to competitors, companies can refine their value propositions and identify unique selling points.

Data-Driven Decision Making: Validation is strengthened by data-driven decision-making. This section elucidates how businesses can leverage key performance indicators (KPIs) and analytics to inform their validation efforts. By grounding decisions in empirical evidence, companies ensure that their strategies are not based on assumptions but on tangible, data-backed insights.

As we navigate the terrain of validating market demand, it becomes evident that this process is not just a checkpoint—it's a strategic journey that unfolds in phases. By strategically employing pilot programs, valuing customer feedback, embracing iterative adaptation, experimenting with pricing, conducting competitor analysis, and making decisions informed by data, businesses craft a nuanced approach that goes beyond mere validation. Market demand validation becomes a dynamic expedition—one that not only ensures the resonance of products or services in the market but also sets the stage for ongoing success in an environment where customer needs and market dynamics are in perpetual motion.

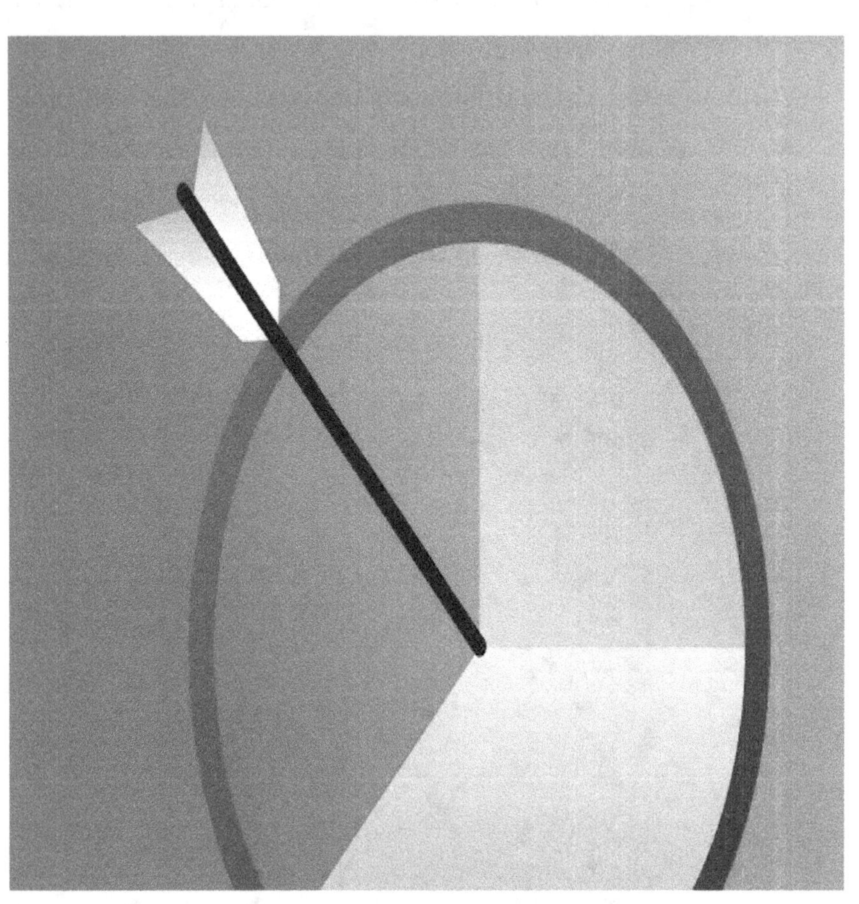

Chapter 3: Minimum Viable Product (MVP) Development: Navigating the Path to Strategic Innovation

In the realm of product development, the concept of Minimum Viable Product (MVP) stands as a beacon of strategic innovation—a meticulous process that enables businesses to introduce a core version of their product to the market with the minimum features necessary for viability. This exploration delves into the nuanced landscape of MVP development, unveiling the strategic depth required to efficiently bring products to market, gather valuable feedback, and iterate toward optimal solutions.

Defining the Minimum Viable Product (MVP)

The essence of MVP development lies in its definition—a product version that includes only essential features to meet the needs of early adopters. This section dissects the concept, emphasizing the strategic decision to focus on core functionalities that deliver value, while avoiding unnecessary complexity that may hinder swift market entry.

Strategic Importance of MVP Development

MVP development is not just a cost-saving tactic; it's a strategic approach to mitigate risks, gather real-world feedback, and refine products based on market responses. This section navigates the strategic importance of MVP development, highlighting its role as a rapid experimentation tool that allows businesses to test hypotheses and adapt to evolving market demands.

Identifying Core Feature

One of the critical aspects of MVP development is the identification of core features that encapsulate the essence of the product. This section explores the strategic process of determining which functionalities are indispensable for the initial release. By focusing on essential features, businesses create a streamlined product that resonates more effectively with early adopters.

Lean Development Principles

MVP development aligns closely with lean development principles, emphasizing efficiency, resource optimization, and a focus on customer value. This section delves into how lean principles guide the development process, allowing businesses to minimize waste, prioritize features based on customer needs, and maintain agility in the face of evolving requirements.

Agile Iteration and Continuous Improvement

MVP development is inherently agile, fostering a culture of iterative enhancement. This section explores how businesses can embrace agile principles, iterating on the MVP based on real-time feedback and performance metrics. The iterative nature of development ensures that subsequent versions of the product are refined and optimized in response to evolving market dynamics.

Early Adoption and User Feedback

Launching an MVP invites early adopters into the product's journey, creating a valuable feedback loop. This section navigates the strategic aspect of encouraging user feedback, leveraging insights to understand user experiences, pain points, and preferences. By actively engaging with early users, businesses gain a wealth of information that informs subsequent development phases.

Strategic Timing of MVP Launch

Timing is crucial in MVP development. This section explores the strategic considerations of when to launch the MVP, balancing the need for speed to market with the necessity of delivering a product that adequately addresses user needs. Strategic timing ensures that businesses capitalize on market opportunities while maintaining a commitment to delivering value.

Scaling Based on Feedback and Demand

MVP development is not an endpoint; it's a phase in a broader strategic journey. This section explores how businesses can strategically scale their products based on feedback and market demand. By incorporating user insights into subsequent development cycles, businesses ensure that their products evolve in tandem with customer expectations.

As we navigate the strategic landscape of Minimum Viable Product (MVP) development, it becomes clear that this approach is more than a phase in product development—it's a philosophy that aligns with strategic business objectives. By defining the MVP, understanding its strategic importance, identifying core features, embracing lean and agile principles, leveraging user feedback, strategically timing launches, and scaling based on demand, businesses embark on a journey of strategic innovation. MVP development becomes a dynamic process that not only accelerates time to market but also positions products for sustained success in an ever-evolving marketplace.

Crafting an Effective MVP: The Art and Science of Strategic Innovation

In the realm of product development, crafting an Effective Minimum Viable Product (MVP) transcends mere creation—it's a meticulous blend of art and science, a strategic endeavor that positions a product for success in a dynamic market. This exploration delves into the nuanced landscape of MVP crafting, unveiling the essential elements and strategic considerations required to bring a compelling MVP to fruition.

Strategic Clarity in MVP Definition

Crafting an effective MVP begins with strategic clarity in its definition. This section dissects the concept, emphasizing the importance of distilling the product idea into its core essence. By strategically identifying the fundamental features that deliver unique value, businesses lay the foundation for an MVP that resonates with early adopters and captures their attention.

User-Centric Design Principles

At the heart of an effective MVP lies a commitment to user-centric design principles. This section explores how businesses can infuse the MVP crafting process with a deep understanding of user needs, preferences, and pain points. By aligning the product's core features with user expectations, businesses ensure that the MVP serves as a solution that genuinely addresses market demands.

Strategic Feature Prioritization

Crafting an MVP involves strategic decision-making in feature prioritization. This section navigates the process of identifying and prioritizing features based on their strategic importance and impact on user experience. By focusing on essential functionalities that deliver maximum value, businesses create a streamlined and impactful MVP that resonates with its target audience.

Lean Development Methodologies

Effective MVP crafting aligns seamlessly with lean development methodologies. This section delves into how lean principles guide the crafting process, emphasizing efficiency, resource optimization, and rapid iteration. By adhering to lean methodologies, businesses ensure that the MVP is developed with a strategic focus on delivering tangible value and learning from user interactions.

Iterative Prototyping for Refinement

The crafting of an effective MVP involves iterative prototyping for refinement. This section explores how businesses can leverage iterative cycles of prototyping to gather insights, refine features, and enhance the overall user experience. The iterative nature of prototyping allows for continuous improvement, ensuring that the final MVP is a polished and compelling offering.

Strategic Scalability Planning

Crafting an MVP extends beyond its initial release—it involves strategic scalability planning. This section navigates the considerations for planning the MVP's architecture and infrastructure to accommodate potential growth. By strategically anticipating scalability needs, businesses position themselves to seamlessly scale the product based on user feedback and market demand.

Effective Communication of Value Proposition

An often overlooked yet critical aspect of MVP crafting is the effective communication of its value proposition. This section explores how businesses can strategically articulate the unique value the MVP brings to users. By crafting compelling messaging that highlights the problem-solving nature of the MVP, businesses set the stage for successful market reception.

User Engagement Strategies

Crafting an effective MVP involves not just development but strategic user engagement. This section navigates the strategies for engaging users throughout the MVP crafting process. By fostering a connection with early adopters, businesses not only gain valuable feedback but also create a community invested in the success of the product.

As we delve into the intricate process of crafting an Effective Minimum Viable Product (MVP), it becomes evident that this endeavor is more than the sum of its features—it's a strategic journey. By defining the MVP with strategic clarity, embracing user-centric design, prioritizing features strategically, aligning with lean methodologies, iterating through prototyping, planning for scalability, communicating a compelling value proposition, and strategically engaging users, businesses embark on a path of strategic innovation. An effective MVP becomes not just a product but a testament to strategic foresight, user empathy, and a commitment to delivering solutions that captivate the market.

Iterative Development for Continuous Improvement: A Strategic Symphony

In the symphony of software engineering and product development, the melody of success is often composed through the artful practice of iterative development—a strategic process that orchestrates continuous improvement. This exploration delves into the nuanced landscape of iterative development, unveiling the essential elements and strategic considerations required to create a harmonious rhythm of refinement and innovation.

Defining Iterative Development

At its core, iterative development is a methodology that embraces the cyclical refinement of a product through multiple iterations. This section dissects the concept, emphasizing its strategic significance in fostering continuous improvement. By acknowledging that perfection is an ever-elusive goal, businesses strategically embark on a journey of refinement, each iteration refining and enhancing the product.

Strategic Planning of Iterations

The journey of iterative development begins with strategic planning. This section navigates the process of meticulously planning iterations, breaking down the development process into manageable cycles. By setting clear goals and priorities for each iteration, businesses create a roadmap for continuous improvement, ensuring that each cycle contributes meaningfully to the product's evolution.

User-Centric Feedback Loops

The heartbeat of iterative development lies in user-centric feedback loops. This section explores how businesses can strategically integrate user feedback into each iteration. By actively engaging with users, gathering insights, and understanding their experiences, businesses create a dynamic feedback loop that serves as a compass for refinement, aligning the product more closely with user expectations.

Agile Principles in Action

Iterative development finds kinship with Agile principles, embodying concepts such as adaptability, collaboration, and responsiveness. This section delves into how businesses can infuse Agile methodologies into their iterative development practices. The Agile mindset empowers teams to embrace change, pivot swiftly based on feedback, and foster a culture of continuous learning and improvement.

Continuous Integration and Deployment

A strategic iteration involves not only refining features but also seamlessly integrating and deploying changes. This section navigates the concept of continuous integration and deployment in iterative development. By automating the integration and deployment processes, businesses ensure a smooth transition from development to production, minimizing disruptions and accelerating the pace of improvement.

Data-Driven Decision-Making

Iterative development is fortified by data-driven decision-making. This section elucidates how businesses can strategically leverage data and analytics to inform each iteration. By basing decisions on key performance indicators (KPIs) and empirical evidence, businesses ensure that the refinement process is not driven by assumptions but grounded in tangible insights.

Risk Mitigation through Iterative Prototyping: The iterative development process strategically mitigates risks through prototyping. This section explores how businesses can use prototypes as a means of testing concepts, gathering early feedback, and identifying potential issues before full-scale implementation. By embracing iterative prototyping, businesses navigate the development journey with foresight, minimizing risks and optimizing outcomes.

Strategic Evolution of Features: Iterative development facilitates the strategic evolution of features over time. This section delves into how businesses can strategically plan for feature evolution, refining and expanding functionalities based on user needs and market dynamics. The evolution of features becomes a deliberate process, ensuring that each addition aligns with the overall vision and enhances the user experience.

Chapter 4: Strategic Customer Acquisition: Navigating the Dynamic Landscape

In the realm of business growth, customer acquisition stands as a pivotal pursuit—a strategic endeavor that requires a nuanced approach to reach, engage, and convert potential customers. This exploration delves into the intricacies of customer acquisition strategies, unveiling a diverse set of tactics designed to captivate audiences and foster meaningful connections.

Understanding Target Audience Personas

Strategic customer acquisition commences with a deep understanding of target audience personas. This section explores the art of crafting detailed profiles that encompass demographics, preferences, and behaviors. By delineating the characteristics of the ideal customer, businesses set the stage for personalized and resonant acquisition strategies.

Strategic Partnerships and Alliances

Collaborative ventures through strategic partnerships and alliances play a pivotal role in customer acquisition. This section delves into how businesses can identify complementary entities and forge alliances that expand their reach. By strategically aligning with partners, businesses tap into new audiences, leveraging the trust and credibility established by their collaborators.

Innovative Event Marketing

Strategic customer acquisition extends beyond digital realms to the tangible experiences of event marketing. This section navigates the landscape of innovative event strategies, ranging from curated workshops to experiential activations. By strategically participating in and hosting events, businesses create opportunities for face-to-face engagement, leaving lasting impressions on potential customers.

Strategic Community Engagement

Building a community around a brand becomes a powerful customer acquisition strategy. This section explores how businesses can strategically engage with their audience through forums, social groups, and community events. By fostering a sense of belonging and shared values, businesses create advocates who organically drive acquisition through word-of-mouth referrals.

Strategic Content Partnerships

Content remains a cornerstone in customer acquisition, and strategic content partnerships amplify its impact. This section delves into how businesses can forge alliances with influencers, thought leaders, or complementary content creators. By strategically leveraging the reach and authority of partners, businesses amplify their message and resonate with wider audiences.

Referral Programs and Incentives

Word-of-mouth remains a potent force in customer acquisition, and strategic referral programs amplify its impact. This section explores how businesses can design referral programs with strategic incentives. By rewarding existing customers for referrals, businesses tap into the power of personal recommendations, creating a strategic loop of customer acquisition.

Traditional Media Advertising with a Twist

While digital channels dominate discussions, traditional media advertising can still be a strategic player. This section navigates how businesses can infuse creativity into traditional media channels, from television to print. By strategically crafting memorable and impactful campaigns, businesses captivate audiences in unexpected ways.

Strategic Direct Mail Campaigns

Direct mail, when approached strategically, remains an effective customer acquisition tool. This section explores how businesses can leverage personalized and targeted direct mail campaigns. By strategically reaching potential customers through their physical mailboxes, businesses create a tangible connection that complements digital strategies.

Strategic Influencer Marketing

Influencers wield substantial influence in shaping consumer perceptions. This section delves into the strategic landscape of influencer marketing, emphasizing the identification of influencers aligned with brand values. By strategically partnering with influencers, businesses gain access to engaged audiences and benefit from the authenticity influencers bring to the customer acquisition journey.

Data-Driven Personalization

Customer acquisition strategies are elevated through data-driven personalization. This section explores how businesses can strategically analyze customer data to tailor messaging, offers, and experiences. By strategically personalizing interactions, businesses create a connection that goes beyond generic outreach, resonating more profoundly with individual preferences.

As we navigate the multifaceted terrain of customer acquisition strategies, it becomes evident that success lies in the strategic orchestration of diverse tactics. By understanding target audience personas, fostering strategic partnerships, embracing innovative event marketing, engaging strategically with communities, forming content partnerships, implementing referral programs, creatively approaching traditional media, utilizing direct mail strategically, leveraging influencer marketing, and infusing data-driven personalization, businesses craft a dynamic and holistic approach to customer acquisition. Strategic customer acquisition becomes not just a series of campaigns but a carefully curated journey that resonates with diverse audiences, fostering lasting relationships in the ever-evolving landscape of business growth.

Lean Approaches to Customer Acquisition: Streamlining Success in Business Growth

In the dynamic realm of business growth, lean approaches to customer acquisition emerge as a strategic cornerstone—a methodology that prioritizes efficiency, experimentation, and customer-centricity. This exploration delves into the intricacies of lean customer acquisition, unveiling a disciplined yet adaptive framework designed to optimize resources and drive meaningful customer connections.

Defining Lean Customer Acquisition: At its essence, lean customer acquisition is a mindset that prioritizes resource efficiency, rapid experimentation, and a relentless focus on customer value. This section dissects the core tenets, emphasizing the strategic importance of minimizing waste, maximizing learning, and delivering value to customers in every interaction.

Customer Persona Development: Lean customer acquisition begins with a keen understanding of the target audience. This section explores the strategic process of developing customer personas with a focus on key demographics, behaviors, and pain points. By strategically defining these personas, businesses ensure that their acquisition efforts are precisely tailored to resonate with the needs of their ideal customers.

Minimum Viable Campaigns: In the spirit of lean principles, customer acquisition campaigns are approached with a Minimum Viable Product (MVP) mindset. This section navigates how businesses can launch minimalistic yet strategically crafted campaigns to test hypotheses and gather real-world data. By focusing on essential elements, businesses learn rapidly and refine their approach based on tangible insights.

Strategic Use of Data Analytics: Data analytics becomes a strategic ally in lean customer acquisition. This section explores how businesses can leverage analytics tools to track and analyze customer behavior, campaign performance, and key metrics. By strategically interpreting data, businesses gain actionable insights that guide iterative improvements, ensuring a continuous optimization loop.

Rapid Experimentation and Iteration: Lean customer acquisition embraces a culture of rapid experimentation and iteration. This section delves into how businesses can strategically design experiments, test hypotheses, and iterate on their approaches based on real-time feedback. By fostering a mindset of continuous improvement, businesses adapt swiftly to changing market dynamics.

High-Impact Channels Identification: A lean approach involves strategically identifying high-impact acquisition channels. This section navigates how businesses can analyze and prioritize channels that align with their target audience and business objectives. By strategically focusing efforts on channels that deliver maximum results, businesses optimize their resources for enhanced efficiency.

Customer Feedback as a Catalyst: Customer feedback becomes a strategic catalyst for improvement in lean customer acquisition. This section explores how businesses can actively seek and strategically incorporate customer feedback into their acquisition strategies. By aligning with customer expectations, businesses refine their approaches, ensuring that every iteration is guided by real-world insights.

Agile Optimization of Landing Pages: Lean principles extend to the optimization of landing pages for maximum impact. This section delves into how businesses can strategically design and iteratively optimize landing pages based on user behavior and conversion data. By embracing an agile approach to page refinement, businesses enhance user experiences and streamline the customer journey.

Strategic Scaling Based on Success: Lean customer acquisition strategically scales based on proven success. This section navigates how businesses can identify successful campaigns and channels and scale their efforts strategically. By aligning scaling with data-backed successes, businesses ensure resource allocation to areas that demonstrate the most significant impact on customer acquisition.

Lean Automation for Efficiency: Automation becomes a strategic lever in lean customer acquisition for streamlining repetitive tasks and enhancing efficiency. This section explores how businesses can strategically implement automation tools to manage workflows, analyze data, and optimize campaigns. By strategically integrating automation, businesses free up resources for more strategic and value-driven activities.

As we delve into the strategic landscape of lean customer acquisition, it becomes evident that this approach is more than a methodology—it's a disciplined and adaptive framework for success. By focusing on customer personas, launching MVP campaigns, leveraging data analytics, fostering rapid experimentation, identifying high-impact channels, incorporating customer feedback, optimizing landing pages, scaling strategically, and embracing lean automation, businesses orchestrate a lean symphony of customer acquisition. Lean customer acquisition becomes not just a process but a strategic journey, where every iteration and refinement brings businesses closer to optimal efficiency and sustained success in the ever-evolving landscape of business growth.

Digital Mastery: Unveiling the Art of Leveraging Digital Channels for Effective Marketing

In the dynamic landscape of contemporary business, leveraging digital channels emerges as a strategic linchpin—a meticulous art that unites technology, creativity, and strategic acumen to reach, engage, and convert audiences. This exploration delves into the intricacies of digital marketing, unveiling a comprehensive guide to navigating the digital realm with finesse and effectiveness.

Strategic Digital Landscape Overview: To master digital marketing, one must first understand the strategic landscape. This section explores the expansive realm of digital channels, from social media and search engines to email and content platforms. By strategically mapping out the digital landscape, businesses gain a panoramic view of opportunities to connect with their audience.

Customer-Centric Content Strategies: At the heart of effective digital marketing lies customer-centric content. This section delves into how businesses can strategically craft content that resonates with their target audience. By aligning content with customer needs, pain points, and aspirations, businesses create a narrative that captivates and fosters meaningful connections.

Search Engine Optimization (SEO) Mastery: Strategic visibility on search engines is paramount in digital marketing success. This section navigates the art of SEO, emphasizing the strategic optimization of content, keywords, and website structures. By strategically aligning with search engine algorithms, businesses enhance their online presence and ensure that their offerings are discoverable by their intended audience.

Strategic Social Media Engagement: Social media platforms serve as dynamic arenas for strategic engagement. This section explores how businesses can strategically navigate social media channels, identifying platforms aligned with their audience demographics and preferences. By strategically engaging through compelling content and interactive campaigns, businesses cultivate a loyal digital community.

Data-Driven Decision-Making: The strategic use of data becomes a cornerstone in digital marketing effectiveness. This section elucidates how businesses can strategically collect and analyze data to inform their decisions. By leveraging metrics and analytics, businesses gain insights into audience behaviors, preferences, and trends, guiding strategic adjustments for optimal results.

Email Marketing Excellence: Email remains a powerful tool in digital marketing when approached strategically. This section navigates how businesses can design compelling email campaigns with strategic segmentation and personalization. By strategically delivering valuable content and offers directly to inboxes, businesses maintain a direct line of communication with their audience.

Strategic Paid Advertising Campaigns: Paid advertising strategically amplifies reach and visibility. This section explores how businesses can navigate platforms like Google Ads and social media advertising strategically. By aligning campaigns with business objectives, target audiences, and data-backed insights, businesses ensure that every ad spend contributes to meaningful results.

Conversion Rate Optimization (CRO) Tactics: Strategic optimization of digital touchpoints is essential for effective marketing. This section delves into the art of CRO, emphasizing strategic adjustments to web design, user experience, and calls-to-action. By strategically refining conversion pathways, businesses maximize the impact of their digital channels in driving desired actions.

Strategic Influencer Collaboration: Influencer marketing strategically leverages the credibility and reach of digital influencers. This section explores how businesses can identify and collaborate with influencers aligned with their brand and audience. By strategically integrating influencer partnerships into campaigns, businesses tap into existing communities and build authentic connections.

Mobile Optimization for Accessibility: As digital consumption shifts towards mobile devices, strategic mobile optimization is imperative. This section navigates how businesses can strategically ensure their digital assets are optimized for mobile accessibility. By strategically catering to the mobile experience, businesses capture the attention of on-the-go audiences with seamless and engaging content.

Strategic Analytics for Continuous Improvement: The journey of digital marketing is iterative and strategic analytics play a crucial role in continuous improvement. This section explores how businesses can strategically measure and analyze campaign performance, audience engagement, and conversion metrics. By strategically learning from data insights, businesses refine their strategies for ongoing effectiveness.

As we unravel the art of leveraging digital channels for effective marketing, it becomes clear that success lies in the strategic orchestration of diverse tactics. By understanding the digital landscape, crafting customer-centric content, mastering SEO, engaging strategically on social media, making data-driven decisions, excelling in email marketing, executing paid advertising campaigns, optimizing for conversions, collaborating with influencers, ensuring mobile accessibility, and using analytics for continuous improvement, businesses embark on a strategic journey of digital mastery. Digital marketing becomes not just a set of tools but a comprehensive and strategic approach that positions businesses for success in the ever-evolving digital ecosystem.

Chapter 5: Metrics that Matter: Navigating the Strategic Landscape of Performance Evaluation

In the intricate tapestry of business success, metrics that matter emerge as guiding stars—a constellation of strategic indicators that illuminate progress, inform decisions, and steer organizations towards their objectives. This exploration delves into the nuanced realm of essential metrics, unveiling a comprehensive guide to navigating the strategic landscape of performance evaluation.

Customer Acquisition Cost (CAC) Analysis: At the heart of sustainable growth lies the strategic evaluation of Customer Acquisition Cost (CAC). This section explores how businesses can analyze the cost incurred to acquire each new customer across various channels and campaigns. By strategically managing CAC, businesses ensure that their acquisition efforts are efficient and sustainable.

Customer Lifetime Value (CLV) Measurement: Strategic insights emerge through the measurement of Customer Lifetime Value (CLV). This section navigates how businesses can assess the long-term value generated by each customer throughout their relationship with the brand. By strategically optimizing CLV, businesses prioritize investments in customer retention and loyalty initiatives.

Churn Rate Examination: The strategic evaluation of Churn Rate offers invaluable insights into customer retention efforts. This section delves into how businesses can measure the rate at which customers disengage or unsubscribe from services. By strategically addressing churn drivers, businesses mitigate attrition risks and foster long-term customer relationships.

Conversion Rate Optimization (CRO): The strategic optimization of Conversion Rates serves as a cornerstone of digital success. This section explores how businesses can evaluate the effectiveness of conversion pathways across digital touchpoints. By strategically refining user experiences and calls-to-action, businesses enhance conversion rates and maximize marketing ROI.

Return on Investment (ROI) Assessment: Strategic decisions hinge upon the assessment of Return on Investment (ROI). This section navigates how businesses can analyze the performance of marketing campaigns, initiatives, and investments. By strategically calculating ROI, businesses identify high-performing strategies and allocate resources effectively to optimize outcomes.

Engagement Metrics Exploration: Strategic insights emerge through the exploration of Engagement Metrics across digital platforms. This section delves into how businesses can measure audience interactions, such as likes, shares, comments, and time spent. By strategically enhancing engagement metrics, businesses foster meaningful connections and brand advocacy.

Net Promoter Score (NPS) Evaluation: The strategic evaluation of Net Promoter Score (NPS) offers valuable insights into customer satisfaction and loyalty. This section explores how businesses can measure customer sentiment and likelihood to recommend the brand. By strategically improving NPS, businesses cultivate a loyal customer base and drive positive word-of-mouth.

Brand Awareness and Reach Metrics: Strategic evaluation of Brand Awareness and Reach Metrics unveils the impact of marketing efforts on audience visibility. This section navigates how businesses can assess metrics such as brand mentions, impressions, and social media reach. By strategically enhancing brand visibility, businesses amplify their market presence and influence.

Website Traffic and User Behavior Analysis: The strategic analysis of Website Traffic and User Behavior provides critical insights into online performance. This section explores how businesses can track metrics such as website visits, page views, bounce rates, and session duration. By strategically interpreting user behavior, businesses optimize website experiences and drive conversions.

Lead Generation and Conversion Metrics: Strategic evaluation of Lead Generation and Conversion Metrics illuminates the effectiveness of sales and marketing efforts. This section delves into how businesses can assess metrics such as lead quality, lead-to-customer conversion rates, and sales pipeline velocity. By strategically optimizing lead generation processes, businesses accelerate revenue growth and drive business success.

Social Media ROI Calculation: Strategic assessment of Social Media ROI quantifies the impact of social media marketing efforts. This section explores how businesses can measure metrics such as engagement, click-through rates, and conversions attributable to social media channels. By strategically calculating social media

ROI, businesses justify investments and optimize campaign performance.

As we navigate the strategic landscape of metrics that matter, it becomes evident that success lies in the strategic alignment of key indicators with overarching business objectives. By evaluating Customer Acquisition Cost, Customer Lifetime Value, Churn Rate, Conversion Rate Optimization, Return on Investment, Engagement Metrics, Net Promoter Score, Brand Awareness, Website Traffic, Lead Generation, Conversion Metrics, and Social Media ROI, businesses embark on a journey of strategic performance evaluation. Metrics that matter become not just numbers, but guiding lights that illuminate the path to sustainable growth and enduring success in the dynamic landscape of business.

Unlocking Success: Key Performance Indicators (KPIs) for Lean Startups

In the dynamic world of startups, strategic measurement is paramount—a meticulous practice that illuminates progress, guides decisions, and propels innovation forward. This exploration delves into the strategic realm of Key Performance Indicators (KPIs), unveiling a comprehensive guide tailored specifically for lean startups navigating the path to success.

Customer Acquisition Cost (CAC): At the heart of lean startup success lies the strategic evaluation of Customer Acquisition Cost (CAC). This KPI quantifies the resources invested in acquiring each new customer, encompassing marketing expenses, sales efforts, and customer onboarding costs. By optimizing CAC, lean startups ensure efficient allocation of resources and sustainable growth trajectories.

Customer Lifetime Value (CLV): Strategic insights emerge through the measurement of Customer Lifetime Value (CLV). This KPI assesses the long-term revenue potential generated by each customer throughout their relationship with the startup. By understanding CLV, lean startups prioritize investments in customer retention initiatives, fostering loyalty and maximizing lifetime revenue streams.

Monthly Recurring Revenue (MRR): The strategic evaluation of Monthly Recurring Revenue (MRR) offers invaluable insights into the startup's revenue-generating capabilities. This KPI quantifies the predictable revenue streams generated from subscription-based services or recurring billing models. By optimizing MRR, lean startups achieve financial stability and predictability in revenue generation.

Churn Rate: The strategic assessment of Churn Rate provides critical insights into customer retention efforts. This KPI measures the rate at which customers disengage or unsubscribe from the startup's offerings over a specified period. By minimizing churn, lean startups cultivate long-term customer relationships, maximize revenue retention, and sustain growth momentum.

Activation Rate: Strategic evaluation of Activation Rate illuminates the effectiveness of onboarding processes and user engagement strategies. This KPI measures the percentage of users who successfully complete key activation actions or milestones within the product or platform. By optimizing activation rates, lean startups enhance user experiences, drive product adoption, and mitigate churn risks.

User Engagement Metrics: Key user engagement metrics, such as Daily Active Users (DAU), Weekly Active Users (WAU), and Monthly Active Users (MAU), offer strategic insights into product usage patterns and customer interactions. By tracking these KPIs, lean startups gauge user satisfaction, identify feature preferences, and iterate product development strategies to enhance engagement and retention.

Customer Satisfaction Score (CSAT): The strategic assessment of Customer Satisfaction Score (CSAT) quantifies user satisfaction levels and sentiment towards the startup's products or services. This KPI typically involves post-interaction surveys or feedback mechanisms to gauge customer perceptions. By optimizing CSAT, lean startups prioritize customer-centricity, foster brand advocacy, and differentiate themselves in competitive markets.

Net Promoter Score (NPS): Strategic evaluation of Net Promoter Score (NPS) offers insights into customer loyalty and advocacy. This KPI measures the likelihood of customers to recommend the startup's offerings to others, thereby serving as a proxy for overall customer satisfaction and brand loyalty. By enhancing NPS, lean startups cultivate a loyal customer base, drive organic growth, and amplify brand visibility.

Lead-to-Customer Conversion Rate: The strategic assessment of Lead-to-Customer

Conversion Rate quantifies the efficiency and effectiveness of sales and marketing efforts in converting leads into paying customers. This KPI evaluates the performance of lead generation strategies, sales processes, and conversion optimization tactics. By optimizing conversion rates, lean startups accelerate revenue growth, optimize resource allocation, and scale operations strategically.

Runway and Burn Rate: Key financial metrics, such as Runway and Burn Rate, provide strategic insights into the startup's financial health and sustainability. Runway represents the projected time until the startup exhausts its available funds, while Burn Rate quantifies the rate at which the startup consumes capital. By managing runway and burn rate effectively, lean startups optimize cash flow, mitigate financial risks, and extend their runway for growth and innovation.

Product-Market Fit Validation: Strategic validation of Product-Market Fit serves as a foundational KPI for lean startups. This qualitative assessment evaluates the alignment between the startup's product offering and the needs, preferences, and pain points of target customers. By validating product-market fit, lean startups minimize market risks, validate value propositions, and iterate product development strategies to address market demand effectively.

As lean startups embark on their journey towards innovation and growth, strategic measurement becomes the compass that guides their path to success. By leveraging key performance indicators such as Customer Acquisition Cost, Customer Lifetime Value, Monthly Recurring Revenue, Churn Rate, Activation Rate, User Engagement Metrics, Customer Satisfaction Score, Net Promoter Score, Lead-to-Customer Conversion Rate, Runway and Burn Rate, and Product-Market Fit Validation, lean startups unlock actionable insights, make informed decisions, and propel their ventures towards sustainable growth and market leadership in the ever-evolving startup ecosystem.

Empowering Excellence: The Art of Data-Driven Decision Making in Marketing

In the dynamic landscape of modern marketing, data-driven decision making stands as the cornerstone of strategic excellence—a meticulous practice that empowers marketers to navigate complexities, anticipate trends, and optimize outcomes with precision. This exploration delves into the transformative realm of data-driven decision making, unveiling a comprehensive guide to harnessing data as the catalyst for marketing success.

Strategic Alignment with Business Objectives: At the heart of data-driven decision making lies strategic alignment with overarching business objectives. This foundational principle ensures that marketing initiatives are anchored in the broader goals of the organization, whether it be revenue growth, brand awareness, customer acquisition, or retention. By aligning data analysis with strategic imperatives, marketers pave the way for impactful outcomes that drive sustainable business success.

Data Collection and Integration: The journey of data-driven decision making begins with the strategic collection and integration of diverse data sources. From customer interactions and website analytics to social media engagement and market trends, marketers harness a myriad of data streams to gain comprehensive insights into consumer behavior, preferences, and market dynamics. By integrating disparate datasets, marketers paint a holistic picture of the target audience and market landscape, laying the foundation for informed decision making.

Advanced Analytics and Interpretation: Strategic analytics serve as the compass that guides data-driven decision making in marketing. Through advanced analytics techniques such as predictive modeling, segmentation analysis, and sentiment analysis, marketers uncover hidden patterns, correlations, and actionable insights within vast datasets. By harnessing the power of analytics, marketers gain foresight into consumer trends, identify emerging opportunities, and mitigate risks, enabling proactive decision making that drives competitive advantage.

Experimentation and Optimization: The ethos of data-driven decision making thrives on the spirit of experimentation and optimization. Marketers leverage A/B testing, multivariate analysis, and controlled experiments to systematically evaluate marketing strategies, messaging, and campaign variables. By iteratively refining tactics based on data-driven insights, marketers optimize performance, enhance campaign effectiveness, and maximize return on investment (ROI), fostering a culture of continuous improvement and innovation.

Personalization and Customer Experience Enhancement: Data-driven decision making empowers marketers to deliver personalized and immersive customer experiences tailored to individual preferences and behaviors. Through data-driven segmentation, dynamic content customization, and real-time personalization algorithms, marketers engage customers on a deeper level, fostering loyalty, advocacy, and long-term relationships. By understanding and anticipating customer needs through data insights, marketers elevate the brand experience, driving customer satisfaction and retention.

Real-Time Monitoring and Adaptation: In the fast-paced world of marketing, agility and responsiveness are paramount. Data-driven decision making enables marketers to monitor campaign performance in real-time, track key performance indicators (KPIs), and adapt strategies on the fly based on evolving market dynamics and consumer feedback. By embracing agility and responsiveness, marketers stay ahead of the curve, capitalize on emerging opportunities, and mitigate challenges swiftly, ensuring relevance and competitiveness in dynamic market environments.

Cross-Channel Attribution and Optimization: Strategic attribution modeling enables marketers to trace customer touchpoints across multiple channels and attribute conversions to the most influential interactions along the customer journey. By leveraging cross-channel attribution insights, marketers optimize resource allocation, allocate budgets effectively, and maximize the impact of marketing investments across diverse channels and platforms. By understanding the holistic impact of marketing efforts, marketers orchestrate cohesive and integrated campaigns that resonate with target audiences and drive desired outcomes.

Ethical Considerations and Privacy Compliance: As custodians of consumer data, marketers uphold ethical standards and prioritize consumer privacy and data protection. Data-driven decision making is underpinned by a commitment to transparency, integrity, and compliance with regulatory frameworks such as GDPR and CCPA. By adhering to ethical guidelines and best practices, marketers build trust and credibility with consumers, safeguard brand reputation, and foster long-term relationships built on mutual respect and trust.

Continuous Learning and Skill Development: Data-driven decision making in marketing is a journey of continuous learning and skill development. Marketers embrace emerging technologies, data science methodologies, and analytical tools to enhance their capabilities and stay abreast of industry trends and innovations. By fostering a culture of curiosity, experimentation, and professional growth, marketers cultivate expertise in data-driven marketing, driving organizational excellence and innovation in the digital age.

As marketers embark on the transformative journey of data-driven decision making, they unlock the power to drive meaningful impact, forge deeper connections with customers, and propel their organizations towards sustained success in the ever-evolving landscape of marketing. By harnessing the strategic alignment, advanced analytics, experimentation, personalization, real-time adaptation, cross-channel attribution, ethical considerations, and continuous learning, marketers empower themselves to thrive in an era defined by data-driven innovation and excellence.

Chapter 6: Scaling Lean

In the dynamic realm of business, scaling lean emerges as a strategic imperative—a disciplined approach that empowers organizations to expand operations, amplify impact, and drive sustainable growth without sacrificing agility or efficiency. This exploration delves into the transformative journey of scaling lean, unveiling a comprehensive guide to navigating the complexities of growth while preserving the core tenets of lean methodology.

Foundations of Lean Scaling
At the heart of scaling lean lies a deep-rooted commitment to lean principles—efficiency, continuous improvement, and customer-centricity. This foundational ethos serves as the guiding compass that steers organizations towards growth strategies that prioritize value creation, waste reduction, and adaptability. By embedding lean principles into the fabric of organizational culture and operations, businesses lay the groundwork for scalable success.

Strategic Vision and Alignment
Scaling lean begins with a clear and compelling vision that articulates the organization's purpose, values, and long-term aspirations. This strategic clarity serves as a beacon that aligns and mobilizes teams towards common goals, fostering unity of purpose and direction amidst growth initiatives. By

articulating a shared vision, organizations create a sense of ownership and collective responsibility, driving alignment and cohesion across diverse stakeholders.

Agile Organizational Structures
The journey of scaling lean necessitates agile organizational structures that empower teams to adapt, innovate, and collaborate seamlessly. This agility is achieved through the adoption of flat hierarchies, cross-functional teams, and decentralized decision-making processes that enable rapid iteration and experimentation. By fostering a culture of autonomy, empowerment, and accountability, organizations unlock the full potential of their talent pool, driving innovation and responsiveness at scale.

Data-Driven Decision Making
Strategic scaling relies on data-driven decision making—a disciplined practice that leverages insights and analytics to inform strategic choices and optimize resource allocation. By harnessing data analytics, organizations gain visibility into key performance metrics, market trends, and customer behaviors, enabling informed decisions that drive growth and mitigate risks. By cultivating a culture of evidence-based decision making, organizations foster agility, resilience, and adaptability in the face of uncertainty.

Lean Process Optimization

Scaling lean entails the strategic optimization of processes and workflows to enhance efficiency, minimize waste, and streamline operations. This optimization journey involves identifying bottlenecks, eliminating non-value-added activities, and automating repetitive tasks to drive productivity and scalability. By embracing lean process optimization, organizations unlock operational efficiencies that enable them to scale operations seamlessly while preserving quality and customer satisfaction.

Talent Development and Empowerment

The journey of scaling lean is fueled by a skilled and empowered workforce that embodies the principles of lean thinking and continuous improvement. Organizations invest in talent development initiatives, training programs, and leadership development efforts to equip employees with the skills, competencies, and mindset required to thrive in a dynamic and rapidly evolving environment. By nurturing a culture of learning, innovation, and empowerment, organizations cultivate a high-performance culture that fuels growth and fosters employee engagement and retention.

Strategic Partnerships and Alliances

Strategic scaling involves forging partnerships and alliances that amplify capabilities, extend reach, and unlock new growth opportunities.

Organizations collaborate with complementary entities, industry partners, and ecosystem players to access new markets, technologies, and resources that accelerate growth and innovation. By leveraging strategic partnerships, organizations expand their ecosystem, diversify revenue streams, and enhance competitive advantage, driving sustainable growth and market leadership.

Customer-Centric Innovation

Scaling lean requires a relentless focus on customer needs, preferences, and feedback—an unwavering commitment to delivering value and exceeding expectations at every touchpoint. Organizations embrace customer-centric innovation methodologies such as design thinking, user-centered design, and rapid prototyping to co-create solutions that address unmet needs and deliver exceptional experiences. By placing the customer at the center of the innovation process, organizations drive product differentiation, customer loyalty, and sustainable growth in competitive markets.

Continuous Monitoring and Adaptation

The journey of scaling lean is marked by continuous monitoring, evaluation, and adaptation—a dynamic process of learning and course correction that ensures alignment with evolving market dynamics and customer preferences. Organizations leverage real-time analytics, performance metrics, and feedback mechanisms to assess the effectiveness of growth strategies, iterate on approaches, and pivot as needed to stay ahead of the curve. By embracing a mindset of continuous improvement and adaptation, organizations foster resilience, agility, and sustainability in the face of change.

As organizations embark on the transformative journey of scaling lean, they embrace a holistic approach that balances strategic vision with agile execution, data-driven decision making with customer-centric innovation, and talent development with strategic partnerships. By cultivating a culture of lean thinking, adaptability, and continuous improvement, organizations unlock the full potential of their people, processes, and partnerships, driving sustainable growth and enduring success in the dynamic landscape of business.

Agile Scaling: Navigating Growth with Flexibility and Precision

In the intricate dance of business growth, scaling up while staying agile emerges as a strategic imperative—a delicate balance between expansion and adaptability that empowers organizations to seize opportunities, navigate challenges, and sustain momentum in dynamic markets. This exploration delves into the transformative journey of agile scaling, unveiling a comprehensive guide to navigating growth while preserving the ethos of agility and innovation.

Strategic Vision and Alignment

Agile scaling begins with a clear and compelling strategic vision—a north star that guides decision making, aligns stakeholders, and mobilizes resources towards common goals. Organizations articulate a shared purpose, values, and objectives that serve as a unifying force amidst growth initiatives. By fostering alignment and clarity, organizations cultivate a sense of direction and purpose that fuels agility and responsiveness in the face of change.

Modular Architecture and Scalable Design

The journey of agile scaling is underpinned by modular architectures and scalable design principles that enable organizations to evolve and expand iteratively. Organizations embrace microservices, APIs, and loosely coupled systems that facilitate flexibility, interoperability, and rapid iteration. By decoupling components and minimizing dependencies, organizations create a resilient foundation that adapts seamlessly to evolving business requirements and market dynamics.

Lean Process Optimization

Agile scaling entails the strategic optimization of processes and workflows to enhance efficiency, minimize waste, and accelerate time-to-market. Organizations embrace lean methodologies, continuous improvement practices, and value stream mapping techniques to streamline operations and eliminate bottlenecks. By fostering a culture of experimentation and iteration, organizations drive operational excellence and responsiveness at scale while preserving quality and customer satisfaction.

Cross-Functional Teams and Empowered Decision Making

Agile scaling thrives on the empowerment of cross-functional teams and decentralized decision-making processes. Organizations assemble multidisciplinary teams with diverse skills, perspectives, and expertise to drive innovation, collaboration, and problem-solving. By empowering teams with autonomy, accountability, and decision-making authority, organizations unlock the full potential of their talent pool, foster ownership, and accelerate innovation and execution.

Agile Methodologies and Iterative Development

The journey of agile scaling embraces agile methodologies such as Scrum, Kanban, and Lean Startup that prioritize adaptability, collaboration, and customer-centricity. Organizations adopt iterative development cycles, rapid prototyping techniques, and customer feedback loops to validate assumptions, iterate on solutions, and deliver value incrementally. By embracing agility, organizations respond to changing market dynamics, mitigate risks, and optimize outcomes with speed and precision.

Strategic Partnerships and Ecosystem Collaboration

Agile scaling involves forging strategic partnerships and ecosystem collaborations that amplify capabilities, extend reach, and unlock new growth opportunities. Organizations collaborate with complementary entities, industry partners, and ecosystem players to access new markets, technologies, and resources that accelerate growth and innovation. By leveraging strategic alliances, organizations expand their ecosystem, diversify revenue streams, and enhance competitive advantage, driving sustainable growth and market leadership.

Data-Driven Decision Making and Continuous Monitoring

Agile scaling relies on data-driven decision making and continuous monitoring to inform strategic choices, optimize performance, and mitigate risks. Organizations leverage real-time analytics, performance metrics, and feedback mechanisms to assess the effectiveness of growth strategies, iterate on approaches, and pivot as needed to stay ahead of the curve. By embracing a culture of experimentation, measurement, and adaptation, organizations foster resilience, agility, and sustainability in the face of change.

Customer-Centric Innovation and Rapid Experimentation

Agile scaling prioritizes customer-centric innovation and rapid experimentation—a relentless pursuit of insights, solutions, and experiences that delight customers and differentiate the organization in competitive markets. Organizations embrace design thinking, user-centered design, and lean experimentation techniques to co-create solutions, validate hypotheses, and iterate on product offerings. By placing the customer at the center of the innovation process, organizations drive product differentiation, customer loyalty, and sustainable growth in dynamic and evolving markets.

Continuous Learning and Adaptation

The journey of agile scaling is marked by continuous learning, adaptation, and evolution—a commitment to self-improvement, resilience, and innovation in the face of change. Organizations foster a culture of curiosity, experimentation, and professional growth that encourages individuals and teams to embrace new ideas, challenge assumptions, and embrace failure as a catalyst for learning and growth. By nurturing a growth mindset, organizations cultivate agility, adaptability, and sustainability that enable them to thrive in dynamic and uncertain environments.

As organizations embark on the transformative journey of agile scaling, they embrace a holistic approach that balances strategic vision with modular architecture, lean process optimization with cross-functional empowerment, agile methodologies with strategic partnerships, and data-driven decision making with customer-centric innovation. By cultivating a culture of agility, collaboration, and continuous learning, organizations unlock the full potential of their people, processes, and partnerships, driving sustainable growth and enduring success in the ever-evolving landscape of business.

Navigating the Gauntlet: Overcoming Challenges in Scaling Lean Operations

In the exhilarating journey of scaling lean operations, organizations encounter a myriad of challenges—obstacles that test resilience, creativity, and strategic acumen. This exploration delves into the crucible of challenges that organizations face when scaling lean operations, unveiling strategies to navigate complexities, mitigate risks, and propel growth with precision and agility.

Culture Clash and Change Management: Scaling lean operations requires a cultural shift—a transformational journey that challenges ingrained habits, norms, and mindsets. Organizations grapple with resistance to change, inertia, and siloed mentalities that hinder collaboration and innovation. By fostering a culture of transparency, empowerment, and continuous improvement, organizations cultivate buy-in, ownership, and alignment across diverse stakeholders, laying the foundation for successful lean transformation.

Resource Constraints and Capacity Planning:
The journey of scaling lean operations is fraught with resource constraints and capacity limitations that impede growth and scalability. Organizations face challenges in allocating resources effectively, balancing short-term demands with long-term investments, and optimizing capacity utilization. By embracing lean principles such as just-in-time manufacturing, value stream mapping, and demand forecasting, organizations optimize resource allocation, minimize waste, and enhance operational efficiency, enabling sustainable growth and resilience in dynamic environments.

Operational Complexity and Scalability:

Scaling lean operations introduces complexities—interconnected systems, processes, and dependencies that challenge scalability and adaptability. Organizations navigate complexities such as supply chain disruptions, production bottlenecks, and logistics constraints that hinder agility and responsiveness. By embracing modular architectures, scalable design principles, and agile methodologies, organizations create flexible and resilient operational frameworks that adapt seamlessly to changing business requirements and market dynamics, enabling sustainable growth and competitive advantage.

Quality Control and Risk Management: The journey of scaling lean operations poses challenges in maintaining quality standards, managing risks, and mitigating vulnerabilities. Organizations grapple with quality control issues, product defects, and compliance risks that undermine customer satisfaction and brand reputation. By implementing robust quality management systems, rigorous testing protocols, and proactive risk mitigation strategies, organizations uphold quality standards, mitigate risks, and safeguard brand integrity, fostering trust and loyalty in the marketplace.

Talent Acquisition and Skill Development: Scaling lean operations demands a skilled and empowered workforce that embodies the principles of lean thinking, collaboration, and continuous improvement. Organizations face challenges in recruiting top talent, developing essential skills, and fostering a culture of learning and innovation. By investing in talent acquisition strategies, training programs, and leadership development initiatives, organizations cultivate a high-performance culture that attracts, retains, and empowers talent, driving operational excellence and sustainable growth.

Communication Breakdowns and Alignment: Scaling lean operations requires clear and effective communication—a shared language that fosters alignment, collaboration, and accountability across the organization. Organizations encounter challenges in communication breakdowns, misalignment of priorities, and conflicting agendas that hinder progress and innovation. By fostering open channels of communication, transparency, and cross-functional collaboration, organizations cultivate a culture of shared purpose, trust, and accountability that accelerates decision making, fosters innovation, and drives organizational success.

Technology Integration and Digital Transformation: The journey of scaling lean operations involves harnessing technology and embracing digital transformation initiatives that enhance efficiency, agility, and competitiveness. Organizations face challenges in technology integration, legacy system constraints, and digital readiness gaps that impede innovation and scalability. By embracing emerging technologies, cloud-based solutions, and digital platforms, organizations streamline operations, enhance data visibility, and unlock new growth opportunities, enabling sustainable differentiation and market leadership in the digital age.

Customer-Centricity and Market Dynamics: Scaling lean operations necessitates a relentless focus on customer needs, preferences, and market dynamics—an unwavering commitment to delivering value and exceeding expectations at every touchpoint. Organizations confront challenges in understanding customer behaviors, anticipating market trends, and adapting strategies to changing consumer preferences. By embracing customer-centric innovation methodologies, market research, and feedback mechanisms, organizations gain insights into customer needs, validate solutions, and iterate on offerings that drive customer satisfaction, loyalty, and sustainable growth.

Regulatory Compliance and Governance:
Scaling lean operations requires adherence to regulatory frameworks, industry standards, and governance practices that safeguard ethical conduct, consumer rights, and organizational integrity. Organizations face challenges in navigating complex regulatory landscapes, compliance requirements, and legal risks that pose reputational and financial liabilities. By implementing robust compliance programs, ethical

guidelines, and risk management frameworks, organizations uphold integrity, mitigate legal risks, and build trust with stakeholders, fostering long-term sustainability and resilience in dynamic and regulated environments.

As organizations navigate the gauntlet of challenges in scaling lean operations, they embrace a holistic approach that balances cultural transformation with strategic planning, operational excellence with talent development, technology adoption with customer-centricity, and regulatory compliance with ethical governance. By fostering resilience, adaptability, and innovation, organizations overcome obstacles, seize opportunities, and propel growth with precision and agility, driving sustainable success and enduring value creation in the ever-evolving landscape of business.

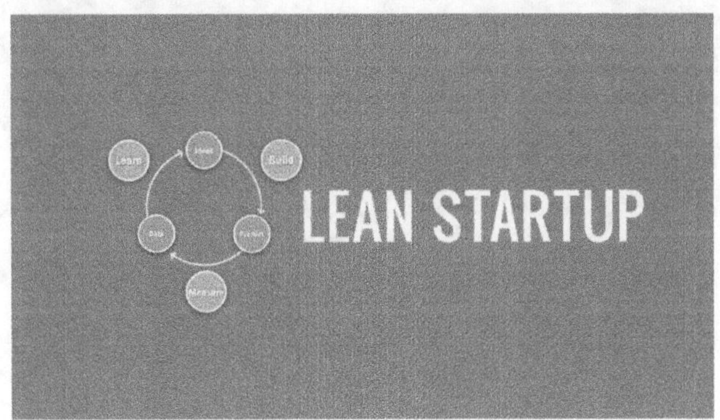

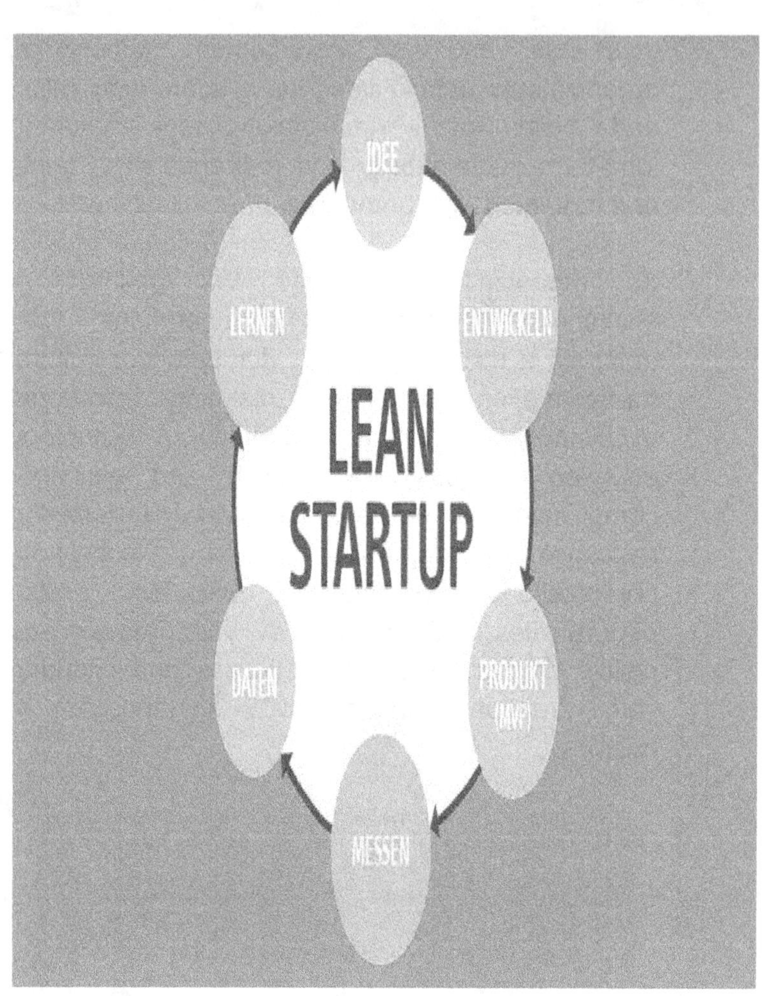
IDEE
ENTWICKELN
LERNEN
LEAN
STARTUP
DATEN
PRODUKT
(MVP)
MESSEN

Chapter 7: Sustainable Business Growth: Nurturing Success for the Long Haul

In the dynamic landscape of business, sustainable growth emerges as the holy grail—a strategic imperative that transcends short-term gains, fosters resilience, and cultivates enduring value creation. This exploration delves into the transformative journey of sustainable business growth, unveiling a comprehensive guide to navigating complexities, seizing opportunities, and nurturing success for the long haul.

Foundations of Sustainable Growth: At the heart of sustainable business growth lies a steadfast commitment to foundational principles—integrity, innovation, and customer-centricity. Organizations cultivate a culture of excellence, transparency, and ethical conduct that forms the bedrock of sustainable success. By embracing values-driven leadership and long-term thinking, organizations lay the groundwork for resilient growth trajectories that transcend market fluctuations and competitive pressures.

Strategic Vision and Adaptability: Sustainable growth begins with a clear and compelling strategic vision—a north star that guides decision making, aligns stakeholders, and mobilizes resources towards common goals. Organizations articulate a shared purpose, values, and objectives that serve as a guiding compass amidst change and uncertainty. By embracing adaptability and flexibility, organizations pivot and evolve in response to shifting market dynamics, technological disruptions, and emerging opportunities, enabling agility and resilience in the face of disruption.

Innovation and Continuous Improvement: Sustainable growth thrives on a culture of innovation and continuous improvement—a relentless pursuit of insights, solutions, and experiences that drive differentiation and value creation. Organizations foster creativity, experimentation, and risk-taking that spark breakthrough innovations and drive competitive differentiation. By embracing lean methodologies, design thinking, and agile practices, organizations iterate on products, processes, and business models, optimizing outcomes and staying ahead of the curve in dynamic markets.

Customer-Centricity and Market Responsiveness: Sustainable growth hinges on a relentless focus on customer needs, preferences, and market dynamics—an unwavering commitment to delivering value and exceeding expectations at every touchpoint. Organizations cultivate deep insights into customer behaviors, preferences, and pain points that inform product development, marketing strategies, and service delivery. By embracing customer-centricity, organizations build trust, loyalty, and advocacy that sustain long-term relationships and drive sustainable growth in competitive markets.

Talent Development and Empowerment: Sustainable growth is fueled by a skilled and empowered workforce that embodies the organization's values, embraces challenges, and drives innovation. Organizations invest in talent development initiatives, training programs, and leadership development efforts that nurture a culture of learning, collaboration, and excellence. By empowering employees with autonomy, accountability, and opportunities for growth, organizations unlock the full potential of their human capital, driving innovation, engagement, and organizational resilience.

Operational Excellence and Efficiency: Sustainable growth requires operational excellence and efficiency—a relentless pursuit of streamlined processes, optimized workflows, and cost-effective practices. Organizations embrace lean principles, Six Sigma methodologies, and process automation tools that drive productivity, minimize waste, and enhance operational performance. By fostering a culture of efficiency and accountability, organizations optimize resource allocation, mitigate risks, and unlock operational agility that drives sustainable growth and profitability.

Strategic Partnerships and Ecosystem Collaboration: Sustainable growth involves forging strategic partnerships and ecosystem collaborations that amplify capabilities, extend reach, and unlock new growth opportunities. Organizations collaborate with complementary entities, industry partners, and ecosystem players to access new markets, technologies, and resources that accelerate innovation and expansion. By leveraging strategic alliances, organizations diversify revenue streams, mitigate risks, and enhance competitiveness, driving sustainable growth and market leadership in dynamic and interconnected ecosystems.

Environmental and Social Responsibility: Sustainable growth embraces environmental and social responsibility—a commitment to stewardship, sustainability, and corporate citizenship. Organizations integrate environmental, social, and governance (ESG) considerations into business practices, supply chain management, and stakeholder engagement strategies. By embracing sustainability initiatives, organizations reduce environmental impact, promote social equity, and enhance brand reputation, fostering trust and loyalty among customers, investors, and communities.

Long-Term Value Creation and Resilience: Sustainable growth transcends short-term gains and focuses on long-term value creation and resilience. Organizations prioritize investments in research and development, innovation, and strategic initiatives that drive sustainable competitive advantage and market differentiation. By adopting a holistic view of value creation, organizations balance financial performance with environmental, social, and governance (ESG) considerations, ensuring alignment with stakeholder interests and enduring success in the ever-evolving landscape of business.

As organizations embark on the transformative journey of sustainable business growth, they embrace a holistic approach that integrates strategic vision with adaptability, innovation with customer-centricity, talent development with operational excellence, and environmental/social responsibility with long-term value creation. By fostering resilience, agility, and ethical leadership, organizations navigate complexities, seize opportunities, and nurture success for the long haul, driving sustainable growth and enduring value creation in the global marketplace.

Building Resilience in Lean Startups: Navigating Challenges with Fortitude

In the dynamic landscape of entrepreneurship, building resilience stands as a cornerstone of success—a strategic imperative that empowers lean startups to weather storms, overcome setbacks, and emerge stronger amidst adversity. This exploration delves into the transformative journey of building resilience in lean startups, unveiling strategies to navigate challenges, seize opportunities, and thrive in the face of uncertainty.

Foundations of Resilience: At the heart of building resilience in lean startups lies a foundation of adaptability, resourcefulness, and grit. Startups cultivate a culture of resilience—a mindset that embraces change, learns from failure, and thrives in the face of uncertainty. By fostering resilience as a core value, startups empower teams to tackle challenges with confidence, creativity, and determination, driving innovation and resilience in the pursuit of their vision.

Strategic Planning and Scenario Analysis: Building resilience begins with strategic planning and scenario analysis—a disciplined process that anticipates risks, identifies vulnerabilities, and prepares contingencies for potential disruptions. Startups assess market dynamics, competitive threats, and macroeconomic trends to inform strategic decision making and risk mitigation strategies. By embracing scenario planning techniques, startups anticipate challenges, adapt strategies, and pivot as needed to navigate uncertainty and seize opportunities in dynamic environments.

Agile Operations and Lean Methodologies: Resilience in lean startups is grounded in agile operations and lean methodologies—a commitment to efficiency, adaptability, and continuous improvement. Startups embrace lean principles such as rapid iteration, minimum viable products (MVPs), and customer feedback loops to validate assumptions, iterate on solutions, and pivot in response to market feedback. By fostering a culture of experimentation and learning, startups optimize resource allocation, mitigate risks, and drive sustainable growth amidst uncertainty.

Customer-Centric Innovation and Market Responsiveness: Resilience in lean startups hinges on customer-centric innovation and market responsiveness—a relentless focus on understanding customer needs, preferences, and pain points. Startups leverage design thinking, user-centered design, and customer feedback mechanisms to co-create solutions that address real-world challenges and deliver meaningful value. By embracing agility and responsiveness, startups anticipate market shifts, iterate on products, and pivot strategies to stay ahead of the curve and drive sustainable growth in competitive markets.

Talent Development and Empowerment: Building resilience in lean startups involves nurturing a skilled and empowered workforce—a team of adaptable, creative, and resilient individuals who embody the startup's values and drive its mission forward. Startups invest in talent development initiatives, training programs, and leadership development efforts that foster a culture of learning, collaboration, and empowerment. By empowering employees with autonomy, accountability, and opportunities for growth, startups cultivate a high-performance culture that thrives amidst challenges and drives innovation and resilience in the face of adversity.

Strategic Partnerships and Ecosystem Collaboration: Resilience in lean startups extends beyond internal capabilities to encompass strategic partnerships and ecosystem collaborations that amplify resources, extend reach, and unlock new growth opportunities. Startups forge alliances with industry partners, investors, and ecosystem players to access expertise, funding, and market access that accelerate innovation and expansion. By leveraging strategic partnerships, startups diversify risk, enhance competitiveness, and build resilience in the face of market fluctuations and disruptions.

Financial Management and Sustainability: Resilience in lean startups requires prudent financial management and sustainability—a disciplined approach to resource allocation, cash flow management, and risk mitigation. Startups prioritize lean spending, bootstrapping, and capital efficiency to optimize runway and preserve liquidity in uncertain times. By embracing financial sustainability, startups reduce dependence on external funding, mitigate financial risks, and build resilience to withstand market shocks and economic downturns, driving long-term viability and sustainability.

Crisis Preparedness and Business Continuity: Building resilience in lean startups involves crisis preparedness and business continuity planning—a proactive approach to identifying potential threats, assessing vulnerabilities, and implementing mitigation measures to ensure operational continuity and minimize disruption. Startups develop crisis management protocols, communication strategies, and response plans to address emergencies, protect stakeholders, and safeguard business interests. By embracing resilience as a strategic imperative, startups mitigate risks, enhance readiness, and navigate crises with confidence and composure, preserving trust and credibility in the marketplace.

Learning from Failure and Iterating Forward: Resilience in lean startups is rooted in learning from failure and iterating forward—a growth mindset that views setbacks as opportunities for reflection, learning, and improvement. Startups embrace failure as a natural part of the entrepreneurial journey, extracting valuable lessons, and insights that inform future decisions and actions. By embracing a culture of experimentation, adaptation, and resilience, startups foster innovation, agility, and resilience that drive sustained success and enduring impact in the ever-evolving landscape of entrepreneurship.

As lean startups embark on the transformative journey of building resilience, they embrace a holistic approach that integrates strategic planning with agile operations, customer-centric innovation with talent development, strategic partnerships with financial sustainability, crisis preparedness with learning from failure. By fostering a culture of resilience, adaptability, and continuous improvement, lean startups navigate challenges, seize opportunities, and thrive in the face of uncertainty, driving sustainable growth and enduring value creation in the global marketplace.

Long-Term Strategies for Sustainable Business Growth: Cultivating Success Across Generations

In the dynamic landscape of business, long-term strategies for sustainable growth emerge as the linchpin of success—a strategic imperative that transcends short-term gains, fosters resilience, and cultivates enduring value creation. This exploration delves into the transformative journey of long-term strategies for sustainable business growth, unveiling a comprehensive guide to navigating complexities, seizing opportunities, and nurturing success across generations.

Strategic Vision and Purpose: Long-term strategies for sustainable business growth begin with a clear and compelling strategic vision—a north star that guides decision-making, aligns stakeholders, and inspires action. Organizations articulate a shared purpose, values, and aspirations that serve as the foundation for sustained success.

By embracing purpose-driven leadership and visionary thinking, organizations cultivate a sense of direction and purpose that fuels innovation, resilience, and long-term value creation.

Investment in Innovation and Research: Sustainable business growth hinges on a commitment to innovation and research—a relentless pursuit of insights, solutions, and technologies that drive differentiation and market leadership. Organizations invest in research and development (R&D), innovation labs, and strategic partnerships to foster a culture of experimentation and creativity. By embracing emerging technologies, disruptive trends, and market opportunities, organizations drive continuous innovation and adaptability that propel growth and competitiveness in dynamic markets.

Customer-Centric Excellence: Long-term strategies for sustainable growth prioritize customer-centric excellence—a unwavering commitment to understanding and exceeding customer expectations at every touchpoint.

Organizations cultivate deep insights into customer needs, preferences, and behaviors that inform product development, marketing strategies, and service delivery. By embracing customer-centricity as a core value, organizations build trust, loyalty, and advocacy that sustain long-term relationships and drive sustainable growth in competitive markets.

Talent Development and Empowerment: Sustainable business growth is fueled by a skilled and empowered workforce—a team of adaptable, motivated, and engaged individuals who embody the organization's values and drive its mission forward. Organizations invest in talent development initiatives, training programs, and leadership development efforts that foster a culture of learning, collaboration, and excellence. By empowering employees with autonomy, accountability, and opportunities for growth, organizations unlock the full potential of their human capital, driving innovation, engagement, and organizational resilience.

Strategic Partnerships and Alliances: Long-term strategies for sustainable growth involve forging strategic partnerships and alliances that amplify capabilities, extend reach, and unlock new growth opportunities. Organizations collaborate with complementary entities, industry partners, and ecosystem players to access new markets, technologies, and resources that accelerate innovation and expansion. By leveraging strategic alliances, organizations diversify revenue streams, mitigate risks, and enhance competitiveness, driving sustainable growth and market leadership in interconnected ecosystems.

Environmental and Social Responsibility: Sustainable business growth embraces environmental and social responsibility—a commitment to stewardship, sustainability, and corporate citizenship. Organizations integrate environmental, social, and governance (ESG) considerations into business practices, supply chain management, and stakeholder engagement strategies. By embracing sustainability initiatives, organizations reduce environmental impact, promote social equity, and enhance brand reputation, fostering trust and loyalty among customers, investors, and communities.

Financial Resilience and Sustainability: Long-term strategies for sustainable growth require prudent financial management and sustainability—a disciplined approach to capital allocation, risk management, and value creation. Organizations prioritize financial sustainability, liquidity management, and cash flow optimization to ensure stability and resilience in uncertain times. By embracing lean spending, capital efficiency, and diversification strategies, organizations mitigate financial risks, optimize resource allocation, and drive long-term value creation that withstands market fluctuations and economic downturns.

Continuous Learning and Adaptation: Sustainable business growth is marked by continuous learning and adaptation—a commitment to agility, innovation, and continuous improvement in the pursuit of excellence. Organizations foster a culture of curiosity, experimentation, and adaptability that encourages individuals and teams to embrace new ideas, challenge assumptions, and learn from failure. By fostering a growth mindset and a culture of resilience, organizations navigate challenges, seize opportunities, and drive sustained success in the ever-evolving landscape of business.

As organizations embark on the transformative journey of long-term strategies for sustainable business growth, they embrace a holistic approach that integrates strategic vision with innovation, customer-centricity with talent development, strategic partnerships with environmental/social responsibility, financial resilience with continuous learning and adaptation. By fostering resilience, agility, and ethical leadership, organizations navigate complexities, seize opportunities, and cultivate success across generations, driving sustainable growth and enduring value creation in the global marketplace.

Conclusion: Embracing the Journey Towards Sustainable Success

As we conclude our exploration into the realms of sustainable business growth, resilience, and long-term strategies, we find ourselves at the threshold of transformation—a juncture where vision meets action, and aspirations converge with reality. Throughout this journey, we have delved into the intricate fabric of entrepreneurship, unveiling insights, strategies, and principles that underpin success and endurance in the ever-evolving landscape of business.

At its core, sustainable business growth is not merely a destination but a journey—a continuous pursuit of excellence, innovation, and impact that transcends short-term gains and embraces long-term value creation. It is a journey guided by purpose, fueled by passion, and illuminated by vision—a journey where organizations navigate challenges, seize opportunities, and cultivate success that endures across generations.

Resilience emerges as the cornerstone of sustainable business growth—a steadfast commitment to adaptability, perseverance, and fortitude in the face of adversity. It is the capacity to weather storms, overcome setbacks, and emerge stronger amidst uncertainty—a trait that distinguishes thriving organizations from merely surviving ones. By fostering a culture of resilience, organizations empower teams to embrace change, learn from failure, and innovate with courage and conviction, driving sustained success and enduring impact in the global marketplace.

Long-term strategies for sustainable growth serve as the compass that guides organizations on their journey towards excellence and significance. They are rooted in vision, fueled by innovation, and anchored in values—a roadmap that navigates complexities, seizes opportunities, and cultivates success that transcends generations. By embracing strategic foresight, customer-centricity, talent development, and environmental/social responsibility, organizations chart a course towards sustainable growth, resilience, and relevance in the ever-changing landscape of business.

As we reflect on the insights and principles shared throughout this journey, let us remember that sustainable business growth is not merely a goal to be achieved but a legacy to be cultivated—a legacy of innovation, integrity, and impact that inspires and empowers future generations. It is a testament to the human spirit—the indomitable drive to create, innovate, and transform lives and communities for the better.

As we embark on our respective paths, let us embrace the journey with humility, curiosity, and resilience. Let us dare to dream, to challenge the status quo, and to leave a legacy that transcends time and space. For in the pursuit of sustainable business growth, we not only shape the future of our organizations but also contribute to the collective prosperity and well-being of humanity.

With this, we bid farewell to one chapter and welcome the next with optimism, determination, and boundless possibilities. May our journeys be filled with purpose, our endeavors fueled by passion, and our legacy defined by the positive impact we create in the world.

9 7 9 8 8 7 8 2 2 6 2 3 3